RAYMOND STORIES

Boston Bar Tales

Raymond Stories
Copyright © 2022 by Raymond Griffin

All rights reserved. No part of this publication may be reproduced, distributed, or transmitted in any form or by any means, including photocopying, recording, or other electronic or mechanical methods, without the prior written permission of the author, except in the case of brief quotations embodied in critical reviews and certain other non-commercial uses permitted by copyright law.

Boston Bar map illustration by
Raymond Griffin.

Cover, book design and story illustrations by
Ljiljana Majkić.
INSTAGRAM: @LILY.MAJKIC

Editing by
Trisha Bernardo and Kate McBride.

ISBN
978-0-2288-5798-3 (Hardcover)
978-0-2288-5799-0 (Paperback)

Tellwell Talent | www.tellwell.ca

RAYMOND STORIES
Boston Bar Tales

by Raymond Griffin

Illustrations by LJILJANA MAJKIĆ

MANY YEARS AGO, when Raymond was a young boy, he lived in Boston Bar in the province of British Columbia. It was a very small town that sat along the railroad track, on a flat bench of land halfway between the top and the bottom of the Fraser Canyon. Above the town the tall dark pine trees crowded round, and below it the Fraser River streamed against the rocky shore. The most beautiful building in town was the Railway Station.

Raymond lived with his father, Pop, his mother, Mom, and his younger brother Allan. His little sister Margaret was just a tiny baby. Pop's name was Pete, and Mom's name was Lucie. Pop had a job guarding the railway and nearby bridges over the Canyon during the Second World War.

Lots of interesting things happened to Raymond in Boston Bar. When he grew up, he told stories about some of these happenings to his children, then to his grandchildren. They all were captivated by the stories of long ago and hung on every word. We hope you will enjoy the Raymond stories, too.

Top: Pop, Allan, Mom and Raymond in their Boston Bar garden.
Bottom: In later Coquitlam garden, Allan, Blackie, Raymond and Margaret.

HISTORY OF THE AREA

THE SITE OF BOSTON BAR is part of the territory of the First Nations people called Nlaka'pamux. Many still live on hereditary lands just south of Boston Bar, at what is now called Anderson Creek. By the 1850s, there was a gold rush in the Fraser Canyon. Gold was found on the river sand bars and among the hills above the town.

Many of the early prospectors were from the East Coast and Boston and had travelled north from the California gold rush when word of the Canyon gold rush reached them. The Canyon town of Yale and the interior town of Princeton were other towns referencing American miners. The locals called them "Boston men", and a big sandbar in the Fraser, just below the early settlement, was called Boston bar. The name became the name of the town that developed. By 1860, the gold-bearing sandbars of the Fraser were depleted, and prospectors sought new gold fields further north.

CNR Station in 2021. | © Darren Griffin

To enable miners to travel north, the British engineers, called Sappers, built the Cariboo Wagon Road from Fort Yale to the gold-town of Barkerville, with Boston Bar as a stagecoach stop on the route.

The Cariboo Road operated between 1865 and 1885, as a main route to the gold fields of Barkerville, deep in the Cariboo area. By the 1880s, The Canadian Pacific Railway pushed through the Canyon as the main Trans-Canada route on the North Bend side of the river canyon. By the 1920s The Canadian National Railway had made Boston Bar a mill and railroad centre with rail yards and a new Railway Station. Also by the mid-1920s, the Trans-Canada highway along the Canyon was built through Boston Bar, replacing the Cariboo Road, remnants of which became "the old road" in town.

In 1940, an aerial car ferry, the only one in North America, was built to provide a road connection to North Bend, the Canadian Pacific Railroad station on

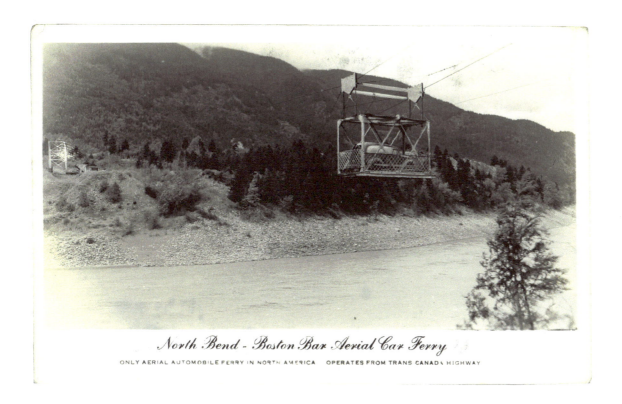

the other side of the Fraser Canyon.

Raymond's experiences were happening during the World War years of 1940 to 1945 when the usual peace and tranquility of the town was interrupted by increased wartime security for the railroad and military activity on the railroad and highways through town. The highway was strategic because it connected East and West Canada, as well as being on the main overland route to Alaska from the United States.

Top: The Boston Bar — North Bend Aerial Car Ferry, 1940s. (Postcard) | © Walker, J.C.
Bottom right: CNR main line at Boston Bar. | © Darren Griffin

Dedicated to my four sons
who so enjoyed the telling.

Family resting by tracks on First Nations land — Raymond, Mom, Allan, Pop and friend Boogish.

CONTENTS

	PAGE
THE WATER TOWER	17
STUNG BY BEES	20
THE HOTEL FIRE	23
RAYMOND AND THE SOLDIERS	26
THE TROOP TRAIN	29
BLACKIE SWIMS THE FRASER	33
FALLING INTO THE SLUICE BOX	35
TRAIN THRILLS	38

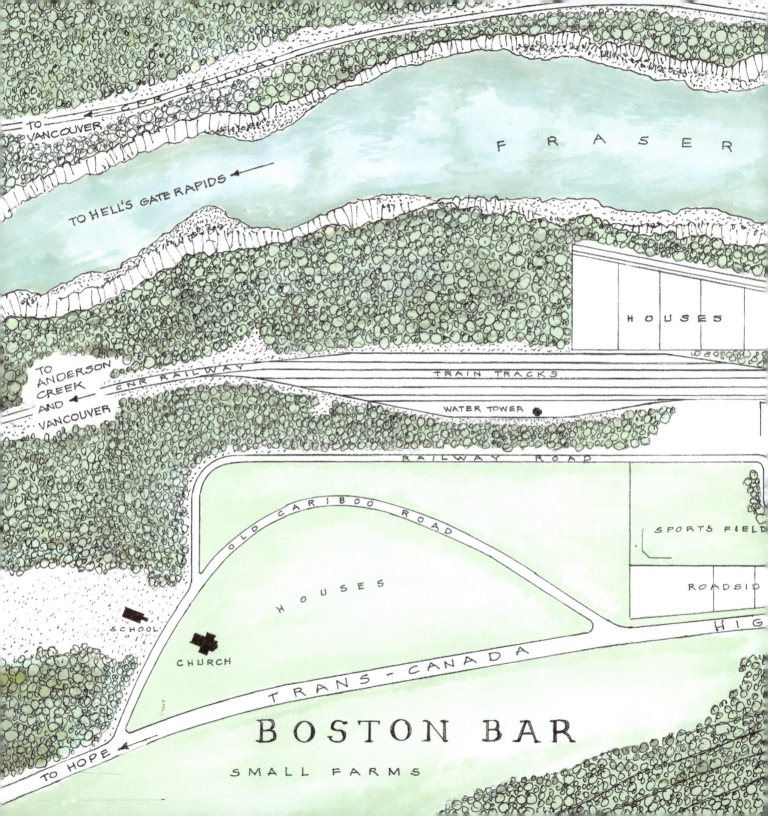

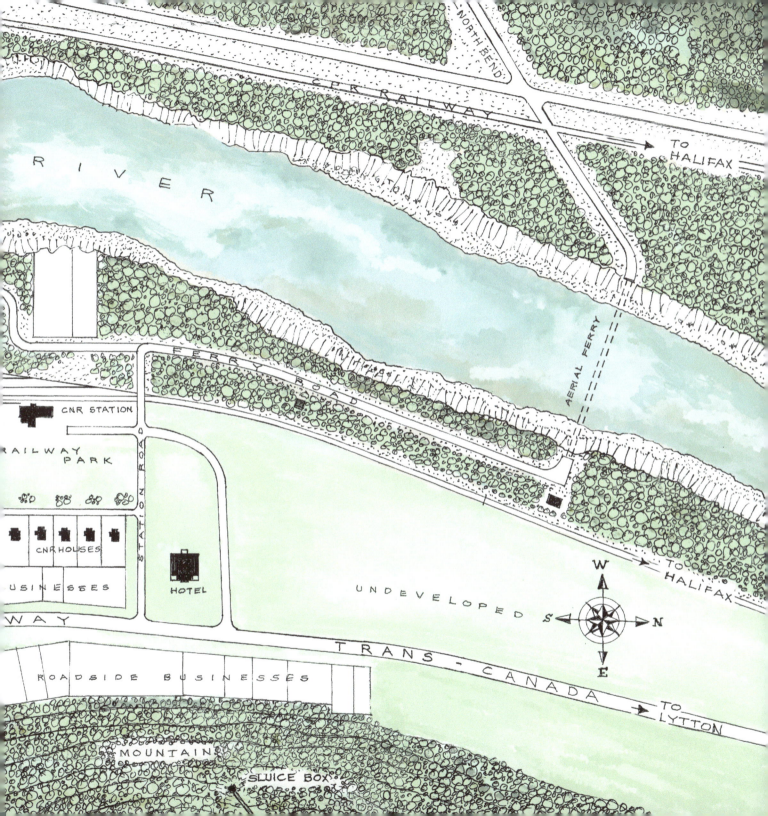

THE WATER TOWER

WHEN RAYMOND was six years old and his brother Allan was five, they lived in Boston Bar, B.C., a small historic town on the river bank in the Fraser Canyon. It was a centre for trains. Near the train station, close to their home, were rows of tracks called marshalling yards. Every day, trains would come through town, some from the west heading east and some from the east heading west. It was wartime so guards patrolled the station and the yards.

A train would often stop at the station. Mom and Pop had told Raymond and Allan not to play near the tracks, but they just had to go and watch. It was so interesting when the huge locomotive engine let off clouds of steam. Then when the train started up again, the giant front wheels shrieked as they spun around. The big gears pushed and groaned until the train started to creep forward and the steel wheels took hold of the track. It reminded Raymond of the local cowboy horses that sometimes snorted and tapped their hooves before they got going.

At the station, the trains took on coal from the big coal bin, or water from the water tower to feed the big steam engines. The water tower was tall, round and mysteri-ous, with large cooling louvres on the side walls and a big snout like an elephant's nose. The snout dropped into place to pour water into the engine's boiler.

One hot summer day, Raymond, Allan and their black spaniel, Blackie, were walking down by the tracks. Suddenly they heard a scary voice from somewhere near the water tower, "Hey, yoouu kids, come ooverrr here!" The voice sounded just like a ghost.

A bit scared, Raymond and Allan crossed the tracks toward the tower, trying to catch a glimpse of anyone hiding there. As they got nearer, the tower loomed high above them and the voice said, "Go to the railroad station and get three popsicles right now and bring them back here! Do it, or else we'll beat you up!"

Raymond had heard that the railroad café had a crazy problem that day: it had too many popsicles. What were they doing about it? They were giving popsicles away — for free!

Not knowing what else to do, and knowing that the popsicles were free, the boys turned back to the café. But on the way, Allan said, "I'm going home. I don't feel like getting popsicles and I'm taking Blackie with me."

Off Allan went while Raymond continued to the café alone. He got three free popsicles — an orange one, a green one, and a purple one. On his way back to the water tower, the orange one began to melt in the hot sun. He started to lick it and pretty soon it was gone. As he got closer to the tower, the purple one started to drip, so he started to lick that one and pretty soon it was gone too. When the green one started to melt, he decided to finish that one off too. By the time Raymond got to the tower, all three popsicles had disappeared.

Raymond was wondering what to do now and thinking about how smart Allan had been, when the spooky voice boomed out from the tower, "Hey kid, where are the popsicles we told you to get?"

Raymond stammered, "W-well, I got them, but it was so hot on the way back that they melted and I had to eat them!"

Then, he heard footsteps racing down a stairway inside the tower and someone yelled, "Now you're going to get it, kid!" Three big boys burst out from the base of the tower.

Raymond turned to run across the tracks back to his house, but just then a locomotive was pushing some boxcars along the tracks behind him and blocked his escape route. "Uh-oh, I'm in trouble now," Raymond thought. He tried to decide which was better: running along the tracks or heading for the train station. He chose the station and ran as fast as he could, but the three big kids were catching up to him.

All of a sudden, a railroad guard came marching up. He grabbed two of the big boys by the collar. "Just a minute, hold it! What's going on here?"

Raymond piped up, "Mister, they were in the water tower and got mad at me for not bringing them popsicles, then chased me!"

The guard said angrily, "You kids know these tracks and the water tower are off limits. Get out of here and don't ever let me catch you here again. And don't ever lay a hand on Raymond after this, or you will be really sorry. And remember, I know all of your parents."

So that's the story of the water tower. Since then, every time Raymond snuck near the tower he wondered if there was anyone up there, but there never was.

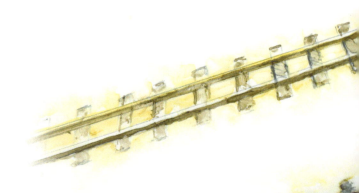

STUNG BY BEES

RAYMOND WAS VERY EXCITED. Today was his first day in Grade One at Boston Bar Elementary School, high up in the Fraser Canyon. He walked to school with a lunch bag, a pencil, an eraser, and a scribbler. First, he found his seat, then the class had its first lesson. Halfway through the morning, they had recess. In ten minutes Raymond made two new friends.

When the lunch bell rang, his teacher said, "All right, children, it's a nice sunny day, so you can go outside to enjoy your lunch."

Raymond and his new friends, Mary and Garth, ran to the woods at the edge of the playing field. They sat on a log, eating their sandwiches. Mary looked up and saw a beehive on a branch above. "Hey, why don't we knock it down?" she said.

Garth grabbed a stick but he couldn't reach it, so Raymond got a longer stick and started poking. He reached it, no problem. The stick went right through the nest and the nest slid down onto his hand. Yikes! Right away, a buzzing swarm of bees flew out and headed for Raymond and the other kids too.

All three screamed, dropped everything, and started to run out of the bush back to the playing field, but

Raymond had a swarm around his face, stumbled, and then all the bees came at him. He finally got back to his classroom, with a few bees still trailing after him, and was sobbing when he found his teacher.

"Oh, dear," his teacher said. "You're in a bad way. We better get you some first aid. I hope you're not allergic."

She slathered a wet baking soda paste all over the bee stings on his face, neck, and hands, and that helped the pain go down. Then she sent Raymond to walk home all by himself, with a note for his Mom.

When Raymond got home, with his face still white from the baking soda, his mother Lucie said, "Oh dear, come on in, how come you're home so early? What happened to your face?"

As he handed her the teacher's note and she read it, he blurted out what had happened on his first day at school, "I got stung — bad! It really hurts," he whimpered.

By this time, Raymond was feeling sorry for himself, because of the bee stings, and because he had been sent home by himself, and because it was all a shock, and because he did not know it was so dangerous to play with a bee's nest. It wasn't his idea to knock the bee's nest down — it was Mary who said to do it and she hardly got stung and neither did Garth. Now he was mad at himself for being so foolish, to just follow a suggestion without really thinking for himself.

His mother Lucie told Raymond, "Well, you certainly can't go back to school until you are better, and it will be a few days before the swelling goes down."

This also upset Raymond, because he had so looked forward to being with new friends at school. She put some ointment on his puffy face, but it still hurt. So Lucie asked a friend who had a small swimming pool if Raymond could come and swim in it to keep his face cool.

When Raymond went to Mrs. Harrington's, she said, "Well, my brave little lad, I've never seen such a swollen face, but hop in the pool and keep ducking your face, and it will help get your mind off the stings."

So Raymond did this, and it helped. As he soaked in the water, he thought, "Gee, I wish we had a pool like this in our own backyard."

Raymond at birdbath at Railway Park in Boston Bar.

When Pop came home, he was amazed at Raymond's swollen face, and when he heard the story, he said, "Well, I have a good mind to keep him home from school from now on, and he can do his schoolwork here. Besides, I'm upset that they did not watch the kids at lunch, and that they just sent him home on his own." Of course, in those days, they could not use a phone to call the parents.

So that was the first day, and the last day, that Raymond went to school in Grade One. For the rest of the year, he did his schoolwork at home with Mom and never did go back to the school in Boston Bar, because that summer they moved to another town, and when he started school the next time, it was in Grade Two.

THE HOTEL FIRE

WHEN RAYMOND was six, he spent the long summer days playing outside in Boston Bar with his brother Allan and some neighbour kids, like Brent from next door. "The Bar" was a quiet railroad town, and the only real excitement was when the trains came into the station, which was every day. Raymond and Allan lived in the centre of a row of houses facing a big green lawn right opposite the Canadian National Railroad station, so they had a good view.

One day, Raymond, Allan, and Brent were sitting on a grassy bank near the Boston Bar Hotel when they suddenly jumped up. Raymond and Allan yelled at the same time, "Look, the hotel roof is on fire!"

This was really exciting, because they had never seen a building burning. They ran closer. Raymond said, "We better go and tell them about the fire."

He climbed up the back steps of the hotel and knocked on the door. Soon a big man with a gruff voice opened the door, "Whadd'ya want, kid?"

Raymond shouted back, "Mister, your roof is on fire!"

The man didn't listen. "Get outta here, kid! Go play somewhere else. I don't have time for your tricks!" and slammed the door as he went back in.

Raymond walked back to join Allan and Brent, and they watched the fire grow bigger and bigger. A while later, the mean man from the hotel came outside, lit a cigarette, and leaned on the porch railing. He saw the kids nearby and yelled, "Hey! I thought I told you kids to get away from here! Scram!"

The boys jumped up and pointed at the roof. Raymond yelled back defiantly, "Mister, we're just watching your roof burning. You better take a look!"

Finally, the man got worried, rushed down the steps, and looked up at the hotel roof. Now he could see the flames. They were getting higher and higher, and spreading along the shingles toward some windows.

The man dropped his cigarette and raced up the steps and back in. The next thing the boys saw was two men shoving a second-floor window open, squirting water and shooting a fire extinguisher at the flames. Soon the town's fire truck arrived, clanging a bell, and careened onto the hotel yard. In no time, the firemen hauled out their big hose and shot a powerful stream of water onto the roof.

Wow! That was exciting! But pretty soon the flames were out, leaving only steam and some smoke, and water dripping off the roof. In a little while, the big man came out again, and called to Raymond and his friends, "Hey, kids, come over here, I got something for you!"

They walked over warily, not knowing what he was going to say, but instead of yelling at them the guy smiled and handed them each a dime. "Thanks for warning me! I should have listened to you the first time," he admitted.

Feeling glad it was over, Raymond, Allan and Brent walked over to the railroad station coffee shop and bought popsicles with their dimes. On the way home, Raymond and Allan met their father and told him all about the fire, and what they got as reward.

Pop answered, "Well, you boys sure did good! But that man should have been really grateful to you and given you more than a dime. I have a good mind to go and speak to him."

The next day, the big gruff man came to see them, and gave them each two quarters, enough to buy ten popsicles, and thanked them again. Word spread, and for a long time after that summer, Raymond and Allan would hear people in the town whisper to each other, "Look, those are the kids that saved the hotel!" and this made Raymond puff up with pride. Now he and his brother were known in town.

RAYMOND AND THE SOLDIERS

IT WAS AFTER A RAIN, late one warm summer afternoon in Boston Bar, when Raymond and Allan came bursting out onto their porch to see what the noise was. They had heard rumbling on the little dirt road outside their house, where hardly any cars ever drove by. First, there were army jeeps and an army motorcycle, then lots of army trucks, big ones, small ones, and some trucks were even towing big guns on wheels, and some of the big trucks had many soldiers on benches in the back. Mom came out to look, and said, "Oh, it's the army. There's a war on. That's why I knit the brown socks to send to the army." They had also heard of the ration cards that Mom had to show at the food store, because "There was a war on."

Raymond and Allan had heard a little bit about "the war," because their uncle "Toots" was an officer in the Canadian army in Europe, their cousins Jim and Fred were in the air force in England, and one of Pop's nephews from Ontario had died in the air force in Germany. One time Fred visited and brought Raymond a model plane to build. But this was the first time they had really seen soldiers and an army! And right in front of their house!

The long line of army trucks had mostly gone down to park in the town baseball field at the end of Raymond's street, but there wasn't enough room there, so the rest turned and came back, pulling up to a stop in a line right in front of Raymond's house, and right up to the corner of the main street.

Raymond and Allan went out to get a closer look and started with the jeep right in front. The soldiers were getting out and stretching, and starting to cook in some pots. A soldier asked Raymond, "Hey, kid, could you go fill this pot up with water?"

"Sure, Mister," and he rushed into the house to get some water. Later, when back by the jeep, Raymond told the soldiers, "Gee, your brake lights are all dusty and muddy. I could shine them up for you."

The soldiers said, "Good thinkin', kid, we'll give you a nickel a light to shine them up." The motorcycle soldier was taking off his long gloves and pushing his goggles up on his forehead, and said, "Same for me, kids, and do my headlights at the front, too." This motorcycle had a little separate seat on the side, with a cosy little enclosed space to sit, and before long Allan got to sit in it for a try.

Behind one truck was a big long gun being towed and the lights on the gun trailer needed shining too.

The gun had a seat, and little wheels you could spin, and they showed Raymond how to look through the aimer circle, and spin the little wheels to raise or lower or turn the gun.

Raymond did a good job on the jeep tail-lights, so next the soldiers asked him and Allan to do the truck tail-lights. The trucks had red tail lights, and white spotlights, and up at the very rear corners had a row of red and green lights. Each truck had a lot of lights to shine. When the first set was all shined up, a soldier got in the front seat and turned them on, and they were very pretty. So one after another, the other soldiers wanted their lights done. Some of the soldiers seemed young, like the teenagers in town. Other neighbour kids joined in, and soon the whole line of parked army trucks was getting their tail lights shined up by Raymond and Allan and the other kids.

> ...the whole line of parked army trucks was getting their tail lights shined up by Raymond and Allan...

After a while, a soldier said, "Hey kids, take a rest, take five, have a biscuit and K-ration."

Raymond tried it and said, "We get this meat too — my Mom calls it "spam."

While they were talking, an older soldier asked Raymond how old he was, and Raymond answered, "I'm eight," but he was really only five.

"Eight, eh? That's a pretty good age. Pretty soon you could be a soldier, like us." Raymond sensed that they knew he was not eight, especially when the soldier took another look at him, and said, straight-faced, "I have an eight-year-old boy just like you back home."

Pretty soon, Raymond and Allan and some neighbour kids that joined in had collected a lot of nickels, and their pockets were bulging. By this time, all the soldiers were eating biscuits and some meat from cans, and some had made coffee from the water that Raymond had brought. Other soldiers were putting up tents in the park across the road, and as it got dark there were little glows from fires from the groups of soldiers, and you could hear mouth organs playing and singing going on, and now and again yells or sudden laughter.

Mom called Raymond and Allan in for dinner, and when their dad. Pop, came home, he was told about all the excitement of the afternoon. During dinner, Raymond asked, "Is Laska in Europe? His Mom said, "Why, no. What made you ask that?"

Raymond replied, "Cause the soldiers told me they were on their way to Laska."

Pop then explained, "These soldiers are American, and they're goin' to Alaska, which is very, very far north of here, maybe four days drive or more. They've driven here all the way from California, and they are only halfway to Alaska. Your cousins are in the war in Europe, and it's the same war, but in the other direction. These American soldiers fight on our side, but our Canadian soldiers are mostly in Europe."

The next morning, dark and early, Raymond was awakened by car and truck engines and he got up and went out to the porch just in time to see the last few jeeps and trucks turn onto the main road, with their red and green tail lights all bright and shining.

THE TROOP TRAIN

ON SUNDAYS AFTER CHURCH there was not much to do in Boston Bar, but if something was going to happen, it was most likely to happen at the railroad station.

So this one Sunday, Raymond and Allan and a neighbour kid Jamie were down on the grass by the station, whiling away the time. Raymond and Jamie each had a penny and they decided to put them on the tracks to get flattened by the train. This was always fun to watch happen and to see whose penny got flattest. Raymond and Jamie had placed their pennies down, but Allan did not have a penny, so he got a few little pebbles and we put them on the track in front of the pennies, in a little row.

They waited a long time, eating the ends of grass they pulled up, until Raymond jumped up, saying, "I think I'll check the track to see 'fe a train is coming."

Raymond went under the fence rails and over to the tracks and put his ear on the tracks like Pop did when he wanted to hear how far away the train was, or if there was any train coming at all.

"Yes, it's coming, I hear it in the track," and he came back to sit on the fence rail to wait.

In a while, they heard the steam engine whistle, "whoo- whoooo," and knew it would not be long. When the locomotive came round the bend, Raymond and the boys waited and watched to see the big engine wheels run over their pennies. They thought it would be a through train that did not stop, but as it neared it slowed, and Raymond heard an older man on the platform tell his wife. "Oh, it's the army troop train from Vancouver, heading to Halifax." The big front wheels were slowing, but as they got to Allan's pebbles, they heard a "pop, pop, pop" sound, and then "slk, slk." As the wheels hit the pebbles, they saw the train driver snap his head down to see what was happening. The engine screeched to a halt just past the station on the passenger platform, letting out clouds of steam. Just then soldiers with arm stripes and rifles jumped on the platform, at the front near the engine and back at the caboose, and kept guard. Raymond and Allan and Jamie were not sure if the soldiers were hopping off the train because of what they put on the tracks, so they decided they better get away from there. As they were climbing off the fence, the windows in the passenger cars were being raised, and they saw that the train was full of young soldiers in brown uniforms. One of the soldiers by the window near Raymond leaned far out,

29

yelling "Hey, kid, commeer a minute!" as he held out some paper money. "What's your name, kid? Can you buy candy in the station?"

Raymond answered shyly, looking up, "I'm Raymond," and "Yes, they sell popsicles, gum and chocolate bars."

The young soldier said, "Kid, we're not allowed off the train — take this money and buy me some chocolate bars, and Raymond, make sure you bring them right back here, unnerstan', and you can keep one for yourself."

Raymond ran to get chocolate bars and ran back to the train, handing them up to the hand at the window, keeping one for himself.

"Thanks, Raymond," said the soldier, "and here's a quarter for you," dropping it down to Raymond.

Then, all kinds of other arms and hands reached out from that window and others, with silver coins and paper money, yelling, "Kid, over here!" and "No, come over here." It was a frenzy. There were too many outstretched hands to do them all, so they just helped one at a time. All the windows were slid open by now, with hands waving all the way down to the caboose. The yelling and hollering got louder and louder, and the bare arms and outstretched hands reminded Raymond of the baby birds in a nest, all struggling to get the same worms from the momma and papa birds. The noise and hubbub brought other kids from the park, and they all started to grab the coins and run to the station coffee shop for candy, and this rushing back and forth went

> **...outstretched hands reminded Raymond of the baby birds in a nest, all struggling to get the same worms from the momma and papa birds.**

on for many minutes until the train conductor yelled, "All aboard! All aboard that's goin' aboard!"

The big engine up front started to do its stuttering, shuttering, and hissing, the wheels began to squeak and the soldier guards hopped back aboard. Slowly, the train started moving away out of the station, just as Raymond walked and then ran along the platform, handing up his last packages of gum and chocolate bars to the outstretched hands.

As the train pulled away down the track, Raymond, Alan and the other kids were sorting all the coins they had got and stuffing the gum and chocolate bars into their pockets. The train platform was quiet and deserted now. Suddenly, the boys remembered their coins on the track and rushed over to check them. The pebbles were just circles of dust and the pennies were flat as paper, and much bigger around so they picked up the pennies to keep. Pretty soon everything was quiet again, and the boys went home to tell their Mom about the excitement at the station, but they didn't talk about the pennies and pebbles on the track.

Mom said, "Oh, that's what all the racket was down there. I could hear it in my kitchen."

There were other troop trains that summer, but some went through late at night, and the ones during the day did not even slow down. There was just that one time, when Raymond and Allan were at the right place, at the right time.

30

BLACKIE SWIMS THE FRASER

WHEN RAYMOND WAS SIX, Pop got a cute black spaniel pup for him and Allan from a nearby cowboy ranch. The cowboy had called him "Blackie," and Pop kept that name. The dog followed Raymond and Allan wherever they went, but Pop never allowed him in the house. "An animal's place is outside," he would always say.

Blackie was a smart dog. Just how smart he was, they found out one day when Pop decided to take Raymond and Allan down to the river. It was called the Fraser River, and there was an aerial car ferry that crossed from Boston Bar to the town of North Bend on the other side. There was a different railroad in each town, so train tracks ran along both sides of the Fraser Canyon.

Pop used to go to North Bend to buy fresh honey from the beekeeper. Sometimes Raymond and Allan went with him. They would visit the Railroad Station Bar and Pop would go in for a glass of beer. The boys would wait in the poolroom and watch the players. Or, for more fun, if no one else was there, they would grab a cue and shoot pool themselves. It was hard, because they could hardly reach over the leather edge of the big table to aim and shoot, but they tried to do what they saw the real players doing.

One day, not long after they had got Blackie, Pop walked with Raymond and Allan down the old Caribou Road to the North Bend Ferry. The name was a bit confusing to Raymond and Allan, because on the Boston Bar side it was called the North Bend Ferry, and on the North Bend side, it was called the Boston Bar Ferry. The ferry was not like a boat; it was more a small moveable piece of the road, with a wooden plank floor, wire fence guardrails around it, and swing gates at each end. A ferryman on the Boston Bar side controlled the motor. Once the ferry got moving, it was carried over the Fraser River on overhead steel cables, like a ski lift.

As Pop and the kids reached the ferry and waited for it to come across the river, Raymond noticed that Blackie was trotting down behind them. Then they saw a sign on the ferry that said: "No horses or dogs." The ferryman told them that dogs were not allowed on the ferry because there was only room for one car and a few people on foot. Since Blackie couldn't go with them, the nice ferryman told Pop he would watch the dog for them until they got back. Raymond and Allan gave Blackie a goodbye pat.

When the ferry came to a stop, the car drove on, and

33

Pop, Raymond, and Allan walked on and stood by the rail looking down the steep canyon to the river rushing past far below. They could hear Blackie whimpering and whining because he really wanted to come with them. Just as the ferry lurched forward, and started its swing out over the river, Blackie escaped from the man and ran over to the cliff edge. He took a quick look up at Raymond and Allan in the aerial ferry, then down at the river.

> **By now, all the people on the ferry, even the car driver and passengers, were looking down, hoping the puppy would make it across.**

Blackie started running down the steep slope to the river bank, but not straight down. He went down at an angle towards the river, aiming ahead of the ferry. When he got there, he jumped into the river and paddled upstream as fast as he could. But the swift river current carried Blackie back downstream toward the ferry. By now, all the people on the ferry, even the car driver and passengers, were looking down, hoping the puppy would make it across.

The Fraser is a pretty wide river and flows very fast, but Blackie didn't give up. He swam so fast that he got to the North Bend shore before the ferry reached the other side! The most amazing thing was, he got to the shore right under the ferry, and after he gave himself a big shake, he clambered up on the North Bend side. By the time the swing gate was opened to let everybody off, Blackie was standing there waiting to greet them, panting and drip-

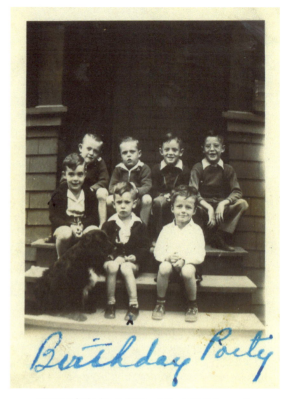

Raymond, Blackie and Alan at Alan's birthday party.

ping, but so happy to see them and they were so happy to see him too.

A man said, "That's a smart and brave dog you got there, Sonny."

Even Pop said, "I didn't think a young dog would know to do that, heading upstream to allow for the current and all, and judging it just right, to land back at the other side, right where he should."

Then Pop, Raymond and Allan went for the honey, and to shoot some pool. When they headed back to the ferry, Blackie was allowed to get on. Every time they crossed after that, the ferryman let Blackie go aboard, because he proved he was a very special dog.

FALLING INTO THE SLUICE BOX

WHEN RAYMOND WAS LITTLE, he sometimes got into trouble while looking for adventure. One time, he was playing with friends along the highway across from his house, when his First Nations friend Boogish wanted to show him the old gold miners' sluice boxes up the side of the hill. "Boogish" got his name from a phrase he used to say a lot, "I boogish that," whenever he wanted something. This was the only First Nations word Raymond knew.

So Raymond, Boogish, and another friend Jamie started climbing the hill, and pretty soon they were among the trees rising high above the little town. Boogish told them, "Watch out for rattlers in here, and if you hear a rattle sound, back away real quick."

Raymond was starting to think this was not a good idea being up here, and he remembered then that his Pop had told him not to climb up the mountain because there were bears, cougars, and rattlesnakes up there.

Nestled within the trees, up the side of the mountain, there were little cabins. Boogish said some gold miners had built them in the old days. One little cabin with a shiny tin roof could be seen between the tree branches down below. They could tell that someone lived there because there was a wisp of smoke coming up from the tin chimney. Boogish said, "You know what would be fun? We could throw a pebble down on the tin roof and see what happens."

Raymond did not think this was such a good idea, because, "They might get mad and chase us," he thought to himself. But then Raymond threw a little rock that landed with a loud "clink." Still, nothing happened. But then Jamie grabbed a handful of little pebbles and lobbed them down. They hit the roof with a "plik, plik, plik, plik-plik, plik." This time, a door flew open and a man came out, barefoot, with red underwear and a rifle! He looked up into the trees and yelled, "Who's doin' that? Come out or else!" By this time, Raymond and the other boys were lying on the ground out of sight, and were staying very, very still.

Finally, they heard the cabin door close. They thought they had better creep higher up the mountain before the man pulled on his boots and came after them. On their climb, they stumbled on a water chute made of big wide boards that came down from the hill above. Water was dripping down from it into a big hole in the ground, and around this hole was a wooden walkway partway down the slope. The boards were very old and silvery gray, and some were rotten. Boogish said, "Here's one — here's an old sluice box. There's gold in the bottom, if we can get to it. Who's going to try first?" Thinking it would be nice to find some gold, Raymond said, "I'll try it," and stepped down onto the walkway plank that went around the pit. The sides of the pit were muddy and the bottom was filled with water, and Raymond thought he saw gravel on the bottom.

As he reached down toward the water, he saw his reflection, and that of his friends looking down at him. Just then, the rotten wood gave way and he went down headfirst, and got his pant leg caught on an old rusty nail sticking out of a board. It stopped him, but he couldn't climb back out or even go deeper; he was stuck. He just stayed still, because he was afraid if he tried to shake free, he would fall into the water hole and wouldn't be able to climb back out up the muddy slope of the pit. He couldn't see Boogish or Jamie anymore but suddenly he could hear their footsteps run away past the bushes. He hoped they had gone to get help or get his dad.

It got very quiet. The only sound was some birds chirping and the water dripping. Then he heard twigs snapping from down below. Someone was coming up the hill. Raymond yelled, "Help, I'm stuck up here and I can't get out!"

Soon there were footsteps behind him, and a man's voice — not his dad's — said, "Well, what have we got here? Maybe a gold miner kid, eh?"

Raymond turned his head and saw a red-bearded man with red underwear pants held on by red suspenders, big logging boots, a rifle, and a big smile on his face.

> "*...if you do a bad thing, it could turn out to be a good thing after all.*"

"You wouldn't be the one that tossed rocks on my roof, would ya? What's your name kid? What'da 'ya doin' up here?" he asked, as he reached down to pull Raymond out of the watery hole.

Raymond said, "My name is Raymond, and I just came up here with two friends to see the sluice boxes."

"Well," said the man, "your friends 'er long gone. They passed me running down on my way up. Boogish should know better than to bring little kids up here. There are old rotten flumes in sluice boxes all over this hill, and if you fall in you can get hurt and caught and never get out. Nobody would know you're up here, 'cept maybe a bear or a cougar would find ya'. With the highway traffic down the hill, nobody would even hear you up here. By the way, I think I know your dad," the man said. "Is your mom Lucie?"

As the man led Raymond back down to the highway, he said, "Yep, it's kind of a turn-up for the books, all right. If I hadn't been woke up by those rocks hitting my tin roof, I might still be sleepin', and you might still be caught in that sluice box hole for heaven knows how long."

Raymond thought to himself, "He must mean that if you do a bad thing, it could turn out to be a good thing after all." But he wasn't sure. Raymond was very glad to get back home safely, and he never went back up that hill, gold or no gold. His Mom Lucie took one look at his muddy clothes that day and said, "Where have you been? You better get changed and then we'll have lunch." Raymond thought this was one of those mother's questions that you do not answer.

TRAIN THRILLS

In the small town of Boston Bar where Raymond lived as a boy, trains were the big excitement in his life. Trains were big and high off the ground. They were long. They were noisy. They rattled and rolled. The engine let off clouds of steam when they stopped. They shook the ground when they passed. They had a loud piercing whistle. To little boys like Raymond and Allan they were like the big scary dragons in some stories their Mom read to them.

Even when trains were not right there in the station, their far-off whistle brought them to mind, and even though the railroad tracks were empty, Raymond knew the trains would be coming down the track soon.

Raymond had a lot of scares, "close calls" and excitement with trains.

Pop, Allan and Raymond at the Railway Park. Their CNR house is in the background.

Raymond, Pop and Allan, on the banks of the Fraser River.

ONE TIME he was walking along the road with Pop, and they had to cross the track. Raymond's rubber boot got caught in the gap between the road and the train track, just as they heard the engine whistle coming around the bend. Raymond tried to pull out his foot, but it was stuck in tight and would not budge. Pop bent down to see, looking over his shoulder down the track, and he tugged Raymond's foot right out of the rubber boot, and they both stepped back from the tracks. Just then, the train came around the bend, and in a minute the engine's giant front wheels were flashing over the boot, and then all the boxcar wheels followed. When the train caboose finally flew past, there was a sudden silence, and Pop went and picked up what was left of the boot, and put it back on Raymond. The top part was gone, from the ankle up, so Raymond walked home with Pop in one tall boot and one short boot.

ANOTHER TIME, when Raymond had gone to meet Pop after his work as a railroad guard, they were walking along the tracks, and Pop said, "Raymond, the train slows up on the next bend, and when it gets here we'll hop on a flatcar and get a lift into town." So as the engine passed, Pop waved to the engineer, and sure enough, the train slowed, and Pop picked up Raymond and lifted him onto a flatcar, then put his rifle up on the deck, then trotted alongside trying to swing himself up to join Raymond on the moving train. But the train started to speed up, and Pop had to run fast, before he could grab on and swing himself up. This all frightened Raymond, and he was so glad Pop made it up to sit beside him, because Raymond had not wanted to ride into town alone, and if Pop did not get aboard, Raymond was thinking he could jump off before the train got going really fast, but then he thought he could not leave the rifle up there. When the train got into town, and they hopped off at the Railroad station, Pop said, "Well, Raymond, that was our little excitement for the day, and we'd better not tell Mom or anyone about this."

ANOTHER TIME, Raymond was walking with Pop along the track, halfway across the Anderson Bridge, heading back into town, when they heard a whistle. "The train's early," said Pop. "We'd better hurry," so he grabbed Raymond's hand more firmly. On a railway bridge, there are cross ties that the railroad tracks sit on, and in between the ties is an open space, so people who walk across have to make sure that they step on the tie, not into the space. It means taking lots of little steps. As Raymond hurried along the bridge, he looked down between the wood ties to see the Anderson River far below. They were still not across the bridge when they first heard the whistle, but now they could hear the train locomotive getting closer, and Pop told Raymond, "We'd better get off the tracks and let the train pass." So, along the bridge, every so often there was a jut-out, where someone could stand to let a train pass. These bridges were not meant for people, but you never know, sometime someone might be caught on one, so the bridge builders had put little safety bays to stand aside in while the train passed, just in case. Raymond and Pop got onto one of these jut-outs, and soon the train flashed by, shaking the whole wooden bridge, and making a big wind that blew at Pop and Raymond. After a few minutes, they saw the caboose fly by, and the train got smaller and smaller as it disappeared down the track, and everything was quiet and peaceful again as Pop and Raymond continued across the bridge to the other side. Raymond said to Pop, "Maybe we better not tell Mom, eh paw?" "Right," agreed Pop.

ANOTHER TIME, a different kind of scary thing happened. One evening as the sun went down, there was a loud muffled sound just outside of town. Not long after, the Railroad Stationmaster drove up to Raymond's house and asked for Pop, "Pete, the freight from Vancouver has derailed; better grab your rifle 'cause we'll need security at the site, and Blackie might help as a sniffer

39

dog." Raymond wanted so badly to go with them, and somehow Raymond got to go along, maybe to look after Blackie, and soon they had driven to the crash site. The site was dark, with car headlights shining on the overturned steam engine, which was off the rails and on its side, with steam hissing above it. Its big headlight was shining sideways and upwards into the night. There were yells. There was an ambulance. There were people with bloody faces sitting on the ground. There were boxcars on their side down a bank — the whole thing was a very scary and exciting sight for Raymond, but he stayed by the car. Blackie was climbing over the mounds, and all around, and he seemed to be some help, because a man said, "Good dog," when Blackie found a man moaning in a dark ditch. Raymond and Blackie were driven home later by the Stationmaster, but Pop had to guard the site until the morning. When he got home he told the whole story to Mom.

The next day another train engine came with a big crane on one flatcar and its own caboose. It lifted the steam engine and the boxcars back onto the tracks, as if they were just big toys. Men came to put the new wood ties in, and pound the new railroad tracks in with big spikes. A lot of local kids went to watch from a sloping bank, including Raymond, who was given a bit of extra respect because they had heard that Raymond had actually "been there" the night before with Blackie.

NOT ALL THE TRAIN THRILLS were from the outside, looking in. Mom often took Raymond and Allan on trips to the Prairies in the summer, to visit her parents in the little town where she grew up, called

Gravelbourg. On these trips, which took several days, looking for something to do, Raymond and Allan liked to walk and even run through the train when it was going. They went from one passenger car to another, past the dining car, past the smoking room, and then back again. They were on the train for days and nights, and they needed to get up from their seats by the window and get exercise. When they went into the little lobby between cars, the sound of the wheels got louder because they were partly outside. They could feel a draft, and sometimes the train lurched from side to side and they had to hang on. They liked to watch the floor joints move, get wider, then come tighter together again.

There was a dining car in the middle of the train, but Mom only took Raymond and Allan for one meal a day. The rest of the time, they ate sandwiches from the large picnic hamper their Mom had brought, and drinks from a thermos.

Bedtime was fun. After dinner, the Train Conductor made up the beds, by lowering a top bunk from the ceiling and making the two lower seats into a bed. On the lower bunk, the window blinds were pulled, and there were little fishnets at the window side where you could put your shoes and clothes for the night.

There was a little wooden ladder that led up to the upper bunk, where Raymond and Allan slept. The sheets were cool linen, starched and stiff, and very nice to lie on. The upper bunk had a low ceiling, and was very cosy. Along the passenger aisle, there were dark green velvet curtains which closed off the bunks from the aisle, making a long green hallway. Before Raymond and Allan went to sleep, Mom said from her bunk below, "Night-night boys, sleep tight." Raymond liked the cool, smooth starched sheets, and the sound and swaying of the train before he drifted off to sleep, and the "clickety-click, clickety-clack" as the iron wheels went over the little joints in the steel railroad tracks below.

During the night, when Raymond had to go to the bathroom, he had to feel for the little ladder, and climb down through the velvet curtain to the aisle, careful not to step on Mom. Then, he had to remember which way the toilet room was, and walk down the green velvet hall in the right direction. Coming back, he had to remember which curtain to open to get to his bunk, then climb back up. Sometimes he opened the wrong curtain, because they all looked the same, and was surprised to see strangers in there, but quickly drew the curtains back closed. Sometimes he would whisper, loudly, from the aisle, "Allan, where are you?" but Allan was sound asleep.

In the morning, the Conductor made the beds, pushed the upper bunk back into the ceiling and put away the velvet curtains. Sleeping bunks became a passenger carriages with seats again. Every day was a new day, and every day the sights and scenery outside the windows changed.

> **Yes, trains could certainly be an adventure, whether when you were riding on them on the inside, or just watching them go by from the outside.**

During the day, it was always exciting when another train passed them on their window side. The noise and flashing images of the other train a foot or two away became a blur, then disappeared into silence again. Tunnels were fun too. Some were short, but some were long and curvy, and in some tunnels, the train slowed down so the jagged rock sides of the tunnel could be clearly seen in the light from the train windows.

Another thing Raymond and Allan liked to do is look out the window when the train went around a curve, and see the end of the train, or the steam engine out ahead, going "round the bend." That was when they could see just how long the passenger train was.

Sometimes the train stopped long enough at a station to pick up and drop off passengers, and Mom sometimes let Raymond get off and walk on the station platform. It was fun to do that, and so good to jump on the little steps, and feel pleased that he made it back just in time when the Conductor rang his little bell and yelled, "All aboard, all aboard that's going aboard!"

Yes, trains could certainly be an adventure, whether when you were riding on them on the inside, or just watching them go by from the outside.

Raymond and Alan on their back porch.

ABOUT THE AUTHOR

A RETIRED ARCHITECT, Raymond Griffin was born in Vancouver, B.C., and lived there most of his life. When Raymond was two years old, his family moved to the village of Boston Bar, in the Fraser Canyon, where his father was hired as a Canadian Pacific Railway guard during World War II. At the end of the war, when he was seven years old, his family moved to Coquitlam B.C.

Ray attended Our Lady of Lourdes Elementary School, and Como Lake Secondary School, in Coquitlam. He later graduated in Architecture from the University of British Columbia and the University of Pennsylvania. Upon graduation, Ray worked as an architect in Philadelphia before returning to Vancouver. During his fifty years of architectural practice, he has designed many significant buildings in B.C.

In his 20s, Ray married a girl from Scotland, Marion Hamilton, and they had four sons. When it was Ray's turn to read them bedtime stories, he tired of reading them standard nursery rhymes and began to substitute his own stories, which the boys much preferred. They remembered the stories when they became parents, and told versions of them to their own children.

Ray is a private pilot, and enjoys curling and lawn bowling, and watching his grandchildren develop. Now that he is a grandfather, he has recorded these stories so that his sons and their children can read about the time when he was a child too.

ILLUSTRATOR: LJILJANA MAJKIC

Watching her father sketch nostalgic scenes and sometimes comical characters in his spare time, sparked the love of drawing in Ljiljana as a child. Before moving to Canada in 2007, she attended classical drawing and painting classes at a fine arts studio in Belgrade, Serbia, which greatly influenced her style. She creates expressive, character driven, strong narratives through multiple mediums, particularly enjoying the spontaneity and unpredictability of ink and watercolour. Sharpening her digital skills over the last decade, brought her into the realm of design and illustration. She received a diploma in Electronic Media Design at Langara College and since then, has worked as a graphic designer and illustrator in Vancouver.

CPSIA information can be obtained
at www.ICGtesting.com
Printed in the USA
LVHW072314010323
740706LV00002B/41